T0171071

UNIVERSAL
CONSCIOUS SELF

SIMPLE STEPS TO CONNECT TO YOUR TRUE ESSENCE

TEZA ZIALCITA

BALBOA.
PRESS

A DIVISION OF HAY HOUSE

Book Layout & Illustration by Cheryl Ticne

Balboa Press books may be ordered through booksellers or by contacting:

Balboa Press
A Division of Hay House
1663 Liberty Drive
Bloomington, IN 47403
www.balboapress.com
1 (877) 407-4847

Because of the dynamic nature of the Internet, any web addresses or
links contained in this book may have changed since publication and
may no longer be valid. The views expressed in this work are solely those
of the author and do not necessarily reflect the views of the publisher,
and the publisher hereby disclaims any responsibility for them.

The author of this book does not dispense medical advice or prescribe the use
of any technique as a form of treatment for physical, emotional, or medical
problems without the advice of a physician, either directly or indirectly. The
intent of the author is only to offer information of a general nature to help
you in your quest for emotional and spiritual well-being. In the event you use
any of the information in this book for yourself, which is your constitutional
right, the author and the publisher assume no responsibility for your actions.

Any people depicted in stock imagery provided by Thinkstock are
models, and such images are being used for illustrative purposes only.
Certain stock imagery © Thinkstock.

Printed in the United States of America.

ISBN: 978-1-4525-8321-1 (sc)
ISBN: 978-1-4525-8322-8 (e)

Library of Congress Control Number: 2013917406

Balboa Press rev. date: 10/01/2013

Dedication

This book is lovingly dedicated to all my children: Jasmine my sweet angel, Matt Anthony Zialcita, Theodore Terence Hill, Tiffany Tresa Hill and Tristan Troy Hill, with your existence my life became a miracle. There are no words that I can write to express my undying love to all of you who chose to be a path of my soul's journey. With that said, I am greatly humbled to be your mother in this Earth. Thank you for all your loving presence in my lifetime. May this book be an inspiration to your soul's path.

Epigraph

"The path of a Master is one that leads to the unspoken truth. It is the seed that lies dormant inside each other's hearts. The way to ignite the fire, is for a true mystic to touch and breathe the fire of God into your hearts, living impeccably with the highest and noblest teachings from the Akashic Records, Archangels and angels and Ascended Masters. May you live your soul's purpose and heart's desires!"

Teza Zialcita

Table of Contents

Introduction

As I evolve as an Akashic Records writer, teacher and healer I realize that these are gifts that I need to share with humanity. The fire in me ignites my heart to help others transcend this lifetime into a more peaceful, loving and joyful existence. Our humanity's evolution of consciousness is accelerating fast and our shift is taking a quantum leap as we speak. Our healing takes place in our unconscious egoic selves and when we tap into our awareness, we become conscious of our illusions. Aligning our ego and true selves which is our spirit, thus activating our Universal conscious selves to manifest our soul's and heart's desires in this lifetime.

We are light bodies living multi-dimensionally in this lifetime. We can achieve whatever we want to create when we are aware of our multidimensional bodies. These writings came to me as I search and thirst for knowledge and wisdom. But truly everybody has their own life stories to tell and whatever directions you choose to take is what matters in the end. Right now intimate relationships within oneself and others is what really matters to me. Simple living, not complicating things but speaking from the heart. Without any judgments about others souls paths we can be peaceful with each other. We can't save the world but we can start by our peaceful state of mind, that creates our thoughts, words and actions.

Our lives are woven tapestry, with all the colours and threads that compose this beautiful mysterious life, we are all one weaving our patterns of creation. As we contribute to the humanity's evolution of consciousness we ask ourselves, "How do I want to create my life?" And if you think you are creating a peaceful, loving, joyful and blissful life then you are in the right path towards your ascension.

Acknowledgments

This book is amazingly here in your hands because of the loving support of these awesome angels in my life. Thank you Alan Hawthorn for the loving support, Thursdays dates and soulful friendship that we have. Thank you Kevin Diakiw, my partner for all the love, support, caring and kindness that you intimately share with me. The dedication and loving support from Cheryl Ticne, my Graphic Designer is just an awesome presence. Thank you Cindy Yu, for your support, beautiful and meaningful contributions towards this book. For all my friends and family that continually love me for who I am. For all the souls that come to my Akashic Records teachings, I express my gratitude for sharing your soul's journeys with me. Thank you Buddha and Gaia, my loving cats, for your presence in my life. Oskie, my loving orange cat, you will always be in my heart.

All of these gifts and blessings in my lifetime would not be possible without the infinite love from the Lords of the Akashic Records, Ascended Masters, Archangels and angels, loved ones and spiritual guides that connect to me. Thank you, thank you, thank you Source of the universal love and light.

Chapter 1

AWAKENING THE EGOIC SELF

Releasing and Clearing Past Life Karmic Bonds

This lifetime will unfold to you what lessons you need to learn and sometimes they come like a pattern of chaos that is difficult to recognize. It is the denial of this shadow that humanity keeps falling into the trap of the darkness. The patterns of lower frequency emotions such as guilt, fear, anger, and many more negative feelings are the basis of your karmic bond.

When you are triggered by someone, be it a family member or stranger, stop and reflect. Connect to your higher self and ask questions to show you what karmic bond and pattern this feelings are showing you. When you ask, the answers are revealed because it is within us. We have the link to the universal mind and divine guidance is always with us. It is in the awareness and remembrance of where we come from that we self-realize our own power and connection to all that is.

The relationship we have with the Source has to be cultivated to nurture and grow this deep, divine connection that we are one and then we can believe that we are loved. Sometimes because of our unconscious negative beliefs about our self-image and identification from our family lineage, subconscious and unconscious negative mind patterns, conditioning and past lives incarnations, we become detached to our true identity which is our soul.

Our life here on Earth is a presentation of our higher self with its highest potential and magnificence. We get lost, and right now is the time to remember who we truly are. We forget that we have the power to declare our given birthright to cast away, release and clear any karmic bonds that are within our energetic fields. With the assistance of our Ascended Masters, angels and Archangels, Star Light Beings our spiritual guides we can evolve and tap into our higher self to shine our bright light.

Allowing this trust and flow with our divine selves, we become empowered and know that everything is taken care of. Surrender to the flow of the universal energy and divine guidance. Let go of your egoic mind and connect to the silence of your hearts. "I clear and release any cellular memories of unconscious negative thoughts, patterns of beliefs, ancient bloodline lineage, past incarnations to be done right here right now, be it done with love and grace."

Steps into magnificence:

1. Trust the Divine connection in me.
2. Allow the flow and beauty of life.
3. Heed the call, listen to the voice.
4. Surrender to what is.
5. Embody love and acceptance.
6. Forgive and let go of negative emotions.
7. Connect to your vibrant expression.
8. Faith in completion of our Magnificent self.

Healing the Wounds of the Inner Child

Healing the inner child is the foundation for healing our issues and dramas. When we connect to our wounds we become aware of what we are experiencing in our relationships with others. The problems arise when we are blinded by our truth because of the logical mind that seems to play the seemingly big role of our ego. When we are hurt, we become numb to our inner self and we project the blame on others for whatever transpired in our relationships. The truth is that we are one experiencing the same level of vibration as the other person. The lesson is within the drama, if you open your heart and mind to what is happening you will be attuned and align to what you truly want to manifest.

Life is too short to be in a space of conflict. It is great to be able to create a life that is fully lived every moment creating love, joyful and peaceful moments with others. To be happy is simple but it takes more wisdom to be in this space. This means to live in the present moment. Seeing the patterns of broken relationships with others and that will point to you where you are wounded. There are unconscious negative beliefs that are hidden and deeply embedded within our psyche and emotional bodies that are not easy to detect. The process starts with questions. Ask yourself to point it out to you where do you feel these situations in your body? Usually your body will answer these feelings with some unusual pain, tingling or some numbness within your cellular tissues that will trigger these memories.

Our body is the information center where data are stored and memories are triggered when it is probed by your consciousness. This information will bring awareness to you where healing is needed. When someone experiences brokenness, usually the relationships between parents are also broken. Awareness is the first step in healing, acknowledging that you have this in your unconscious will bring this fully into your conscious field of awareness. Letting go of pain and allowing forgiveness will put you in the space for healing. As long as you hold resentment and unforgiveness for others, it will not bring any peace for you because of the attachment to the energetic link to the other party. True freedom is about this release of pain and establishing forgiveness for others and yourselves for whatever transpires in the past. This is the new path of healing your soul and wounded inner child.

We are here to experience love, peace and joy, but our lives became more complicated when we are born with imperfect and broken parents. We learn to distrust this world and become victims of circumstances. We disempower ourselves and forget our true natural state, which is love. Separation becomes our identity, and our ego plays a big part in our false identity. When our space is about love we create more love and there is no space for fear or pain. This is what we need in this world, if we feel this way we will not have war or separation. It starts within ourselves, when we feel we are loved we know how to love others for who they truly are.

Steps in Healing the Inner Child:

1. Awareness of your broken relationships and what is the theme or recurring pattern of these dramas?
2. Reflecting back in your childhood, ask yourself what are the painful experiences with your parents and family members?
3. Be attune with your physical body and how you feel about these sensations when you ask your self which body part you are feeling these past experiences? You will feel where your energy is stuck in your body parts.
4. Forgiveness for yourself and others will release you from holding this stuck energy between your past and the now moment.
5. Releasing the past and allowing yourself to go with flow of the universal energy will open new doors of opportunities for manifesting what your heart desires.
6. Spend time with your inner child, remember the things that made you happy when you were small, and recreate these loving moments with your inner child. This is what we call adopting the child in you that felt abandoned.
7. Be happy and start where you are. Whatever state you are in right now, be kind and compassionate with yourself. This is the space of love that you

want to manifest fully into your essence. To be able to feel loved and be loved for who you truly are. The "I am" presence where there is no ego playing big and knowing that you are more than what your mind thinks. This is you recreating the innocence, playful and loving nature of your inner child. Bring your inner child in alignment with yourself right here in the space of love and blissful peace.

Healing Roots of Anger

What is anger? It is a space of separation from your truth which is love, oneness and peace. It is a projection of your separation from the other person or thing that you are angry about. An emotion that triggers deeper part of the collective underlying emotions that are the root causes of this emotion to surface. We have to examine these emotions underlying within us to know why we are angry and how we can heal our anger requires inner work and reflection.

As I've observed the faces of anger, I realized that there is a passive and active action that happens when anger is expressed. There is the passive or repressed anger that someone goes through. One is unconscious about this because they tend to go into their own shell that they repressed or suppressed their emotions and find themselves isolated and withdrawn from the other person who is on the receiver side. They clam up and this is the way they express their anger towards the other person without knowing that they are doing this passive approach to anger. This is about control and manipulation of emotion that they withhold their openness in order not to share their true feelings. Disconnected from the other person and their own emotional body, they learn to close their heart. This state mostly happens to abused vulnerable victims and they need to empower themselves by tuning into their emotional body and release this pain and how they cope or voice their anger.

The other face of anger is the aggressive volatile approach and this can be threatening to relationships to people that you love the most because it breeds fear, anxiety and mistrust. An explosive energy is triggered when one is not aware of their pain body. The person is blind to his reality and it destroys your inner peace which gives way to a cycle of guilt, regret and leads to more frustrations and anger. It is a projection of your pain body and separation from your oneness state of well being. Take this as a catalyst to find the root cause of your anger, for healing your soul.

You are holding to the old structure of belief about yourself and others. There is no separation of our self and others, so if you are angry at others you are also angry at yourself. We are all one. There is a story that you are holding in the unconscious state of negative vibrations that leads to anger. Being hard on yourself and not forgiving others for the pain that they had caused you in the past. Relieving this emotion in your present moment with situations that arises. The universe will always give these windows of opportunities to practice your anger management.

> *Anger creates hostility, conflicts and stress that limit your potential to experience true love.*

This is not the space someone wants to be, we all want to be loved. But somehow we forget how, and we seem to know and do the things that do not promote love but breeds hatred. Awareness of this emotion can help transcend your life. When you become the observer or witness to the situation then you will find a space to go to instead of reacting and experiencing anger. This is the state of suspension, like a hanging bridge towards peace. Use this emotion as an opportunity for spiritual awakening, in that state of powerlessness be the Awareness that arises.

Your presence will be more pronounced as these situations give you more doors of opportunities to practice and be the master of your anger. These emotions are not you; do not identify with them. They are powerless when you become the awareness itself. There is no more meaning and no reactions to these thoughts that triggers anger. You just become the space of Oneness, where there is no separation of others and yourself.

Healthy steps to take when feeling angry:

1. Recognize your emotions when you are angry, stay in the emotional body and feel them (ie. frustrations, anxiety, adrenalin rush).

2. Breathe, breathe, breathe then you know that you have arrived in the space of suspension like a hanging bridge between turmoil or inner peace.

3. Give yourself a space and open the communication between two parties when ready to be the observer or witness to your awareness.

4. Take this door of opportunity for openness and loving communication between two souls.

5. Stay in your heart space, be vulnerable, honest about your feelings, and know that you are always safe and loved in this space that you had become a participant in the universal fields.

Bless this opportunity that helps you transcend your emotional state of separation into Oneness with other sentient beings. As you create this awareness you create a rippling effect in the collective consciousness of humanity towards peace and not war. We have to be aware of our inner peace in order to shift our state into Oneness. Be the peace you want to be.

Emotions That Block Our Ascension

In our soul journey towards ascension, what blocks us in this process are the emotions that are toxic in our growth and healing. If we want to grow, ascend and be one with the Source of life and love, we have to be aware of our vibrations in our emotional fields. Some people are stuck in their own emotional body because they don't want to face their fears and they run away analysing in denial of their own shadows. You can never run away from your own emotional body because you attract situations in the universal energy that give you the same situation but different drama so to speak.

> *Listen with your heart open and know that what is presented to you even if it's negative is a lesson to be learned.*

When you have an open mind and are accepting where you are right now, you open a window of opportunity that will allow your growth to happen. Just like a seed in the ground, it will take roots and become a tree when the breakthrough happens. We are living inside our head and we forget that our heart is the access to our truth and freedom. We attain liberation from our own created illusions and fears.

There is nothing to be afraid of and the shadows that we create are an escape from our truth. We want to be in the dark because we don't want to see our own light and brightness. The responsibility that we have when we hold this light is overwhelming to us because we know that when we have this torch, we cannot go back. We are given this gift of light to shine to others illuminating what they have forgotten about themselves, their truth and what really matters in this world. When we see our relationships to others as our own self we become Oneness. When we reach this point of clarity that whatever we see with others is an aspect of our own self is when you can feel that you have attain this beautiful light of divine love. The deep compassion and kindness for others without judgement and just is. Unconditional love, forgiving others for their mistakes and allowing them to grow in their own soul's journey.

The undesired negative emotions such as anger, guilt, unforgiveness, arrogance, anxiety, fear, separation, judgment, greed, and many others attract drama and sufferings. Our natural state is love and light, when we carry these negative vibrations, we carry heaviness and density within our energetic fields. This will result to stress, illness and death of our cells because our cellular tissues, fibre, memories and consciousness reacts to our emotional vibratory frequency as they emit electrical energy in our circulatory system that regulates our heart and heart chakra energy system. Therefore the emotional blockage can result in our detrimental state of condition when we are not aware of what we are carrying in our emotional energy.

Everything is interconnected.

Every cell in our body emits information and codes to function in harmonized and synchronized systems. Awareness of our emotions and what they carry in our vibrations and consciousness will enhance our existence. It will help us get back to homeostasis and balance our flow within our body and our energetic fields.

We have to release and clear our consciousness from these toxic emotions in order to move forward. We don't want to get stuck in the cycle of victim consciousness but we want to empower ourselves and be aligned with our universal soul's purpose. We are born to be big, expand your knowledge by tapping into the universal mind of God and your Akashic Records. By doing this you will attain your blissful space of unconditional love and compassion for humanity and all beings.

Together we will create a beautiful and peaceful world with the Universe.

We are here to experience unification of our mind, body, spirit and souls. We exist in all multi dimensional states of consciousness when we are open to all that is. We carry this in our DNA codes that we forget, we are here to remember our divine link to God. We become the co creator of our blueprints, when we open these doors of communication within our hearts and others. We are all One in love and light. When we feel separated, we need to look within ourselves, and ask, "Where in my body do I feel separated?" This will lead you to the answer because others is but an aspect of your own self. The illusion is the separation, when you find the answer that we are just one aspect or fragmented part of our selves then you are one with the Source. You become at peace with yourself and others. This is the true definition of oneness. When the relationships that we build around us is about unconditional love, forgiveness, compassion and kindness. May this light shine upon your heart and mind, align you to the greater source and power of divine love and light!

How Can We Lift Our Negative Emotions?

Negative emotions carry a lot of lower frequency vibrations in our energetic fields. When we vibrate in these lover vibrations we attract drama, pain and suffering. Why do people like to suffer? Because they are not aware of their true essence which is Light and Love. There is a separation between themselves and others. They have not awakened and unveiled the truth that what they perceive from others is who they are inside themselves. Others are mirrors of themselves and if they take the time to ask themselves and reflect about what they don't like with others. They would find the answers right in their eyes.

When someone is not awake, they think that others are doing things to them and they become the victims. They react to others manipulations and become a part of the power struggle. They lose their true identity which is their essence or soul. These emotions are dragging them down because of the negative effects in their body. Truth calibrates in their true nature and this creates physical wellness in their health and well-being.

When you are not in in your highest self you create stress which manifest in our physical bodies such as pain and other symptoms of diseases. The separation from others is coming from unconscious self, when we wake up and find that we are all one in this field of energy, everything becomes one in our eyes and we flow with the universal energy. We tune into the music of our soul and we become aware of our magnificent power and connection.

Simple steps on how to lift your negative emotions:

1. Feel your emotions and ask yourself what are my feelings right now? When you ask yourself, you become aware, connected and present with your heart consciousness.
2. Breathe, reflect and ask yourself, where is this feeling coming from the past experiences? Most patterns of negative emotions are triggers of unhealed wounds from the past like childhood. Connecting them will bring healing and self-realization that you are carrying emotional traumas from childhood that yet to be healed.
3. Be loving and kind to yourself. Don't drag yourself down into the abyss of darkness. Remind yourself that everything passes away. Connect to nature and walk, allowing steps to move forward and clear your mind from thoughts that are not for your highest good.
4. Serve others, share your gifts and this will help you stay positive in your down times. Giving and receiving love from others generates more feelings of abundance and positive emotions.

We go through this process as human beings. Our blueprints have these experiences when we come into this world. We are remembering our true selves in these multidimensional shifts right now in our evolution of human consciousness. We are accessing the path to the heart of the Akashic Records that holds our book of life. When you tap into your soul Records, you evolve and shift your perceptions on how you view your life's experiences. There are awakenings that are happening right now that people are remembering who they truly are. Let us help others transcend their sufferings by being the love and light that we are. Shine your positive self!

Chapter 2

AWARENESS OF OUR ILLUSIONS

The Power of Lifting the Veil of Illusion

Relationships are tools to guide you in what you needed to see about yourself. The experiences that you had as a child were programmed into your subconscious that you are not aware. These dramas or schema will trigger your fears and you will only be aware of these subtle signs when you truly open your heart and mind to healing. The heart opens like a lotus ready to bloom into its beautiful presence from the muddy Earth.

The cycle of our negative patterns is a clear indication of our unresolved emotional and mental wounds. The ones that you attract into your relationships are people that will point to you what you need to heal. This is not easy to detect because we look at the dramas as separate from us. We tend to blame or see others as separate from ourselves so the problems become theirs not ours. We then trigger our coping mechanisms such as flight or flee. Running away from our problems is never going to solve what we are trying to heal. Our mind is not built to solve with the same mind that created the problem. Unless we heal our consciousness and see that everything that is in our energetic fields is our creation then we cannot see what we need to heal. Our physical realities are our projections, therefore we are responsible for all our creations and manifestations. Our ego, emotions and mental thoughts destruct us from the flow of our soul's evolution. But if you take these blockages as tools to achieve happiness and healing we can become empower and see beyond the veil of illusions.

Acceptance of our self is the first step into knowing our wounds. When we see others just like us, like mirrors, then we realize we are the same. We will know more about ourselves and others, that truly we are just one fragmented part of our souls. Growing up with criticism, I realized that I judge others easily. When I stop judging myself and just allow this self-love to grow and see others as parts of myself, I become One with all that is. I learn to accept myself with unconditional love.

Allowing the flow of life will take you into your path of healing, when you listen to what the universe is telling you.

Listening takes stillness of the mind, reflection and aligning your mind with your heart's desires. Happiness is achieve when someone abides in the present moment and knows that everything passes away. Peace and joy will be there when someone becomes one with themselves. Whatever emotion is revealed to you, connect, feel and ask yourself where is these coming from? When we ask we connect to the mysteries of the universe, we are given the answers from within and our higher self which is our soul. We become align to our heart's desires.

Trusting that there is light in the midst of darkness will give you faith into a new and expansive universal mind that you connect. This new energy of happiness and bliss will transmute all that is not of light or vibrating in the lower frequencies of negative emotions of fear. Love is the answer to healing our fears. This is not achieved until someone realizes that love is within and self-love will be the first step into our healing. When I ask this question, "If I truly love myself, what would I be doing in this situation?" I get the answers because I connect to loving myself.

Whatever state you are in is where you are supposed to be. Accept and allow this flow and let the divine energy of love heals your soul. This is your lifetime and you are here to experience love and happiness. Become the co-creator of your dreams with so much love, abundance and happiness that we have in our hands, when we take the time to see beyond the fears and illusions of our ego. Let's lift these veils and empower our souls in this lifetime.

Viewing Projections

When you are awake and aware that all your realities are projections of your consciousness, you become cognizant of where you are. Awareness is a gift to know how to shift from negative to positive outlook in life. There is light in every darkness. When you shine light into any situations, dark dissipates.

Relationships with others, they are here to point to us where we are in our consciousness. When we are one with all that is, the Tao, Source, Higher Power, or God we are enlightened sentient beings. We radiate this beautiful light of love and compassion for all other beings. We become one with all that. Be a guide for others to see the light.

How we see the world is what we experience in our lifetime. When we become aware of this, we then get the chance to shift our perceptions beyond the level of our understanding. Consciousness is the root of our realities. We have to uproot our old beliefs and memories to create new patterns of living. As we evolve in our existence, we become connected to the Source and create miracles along the way. Everything is energy, be aware of your vibrations to help you connect to your highest self.

Connecting to your higher Self is aligning to the Source. Creativity is the path to true joy and bliss. When we are align to our highest potential we are connecting to our passion. There is a fire that ignites within our hearts and connects us to no space and time. We are omnipresent, omnipotent and omniscient beings that choose to be here to experience beautiful things.

Create and connect to your lovely self by being aware of your emotional and mental fields. These will direct you within and look deeper into your consciousness to see where you can change or transform your realities by switching your vibrations.

Clearing your energetic fields, unconscious negative beliefs, karmic bonds, attachments and activating your cellular memories and consciousness to your truth or light will help you in your shift of evolution. The Sacred geometrical patterns that are here to help you in creating new patterns of thoughts and consciousness is important in this human evolution. The fields are in your hands to align yourself to your Universal self. You are the universe. You have the power to create whatever you choose to. See your realities as the mirrors of your perceptions and when you don't like what you see, shift and align to your highest self.

> *View your projections as your guide to what is inside of you.*

The picture that you paint is your colourful world, paint with beautiful and lively colours like the collection of vibrant colours in the art mosaic. You are the artist of your dream. Dream and see with the lenses of the Source and you will find that everything makes sense in the bigger picture.

Unveiling the Pain from Your Heart

Unmasking these layers of pain in your heart is a process of being true to yourself. When you face your fear of unveiling the truth, unconditional love for yourself comes through. There is no hidden truth only what is felt within your heart. Open the doorway of your heart and listen to what it says.

Receive, don't resist. Let the flow of light penetrate its shadows of fear. This fear of intimacy is the mask covering the walls around your heart. When it reveals the pain that underlies the core patterns of suffering, it is easier to breathe and allow the deepest healing of your heart. The pain that lingers and calls for attention suddenly comes into a still and holds the space of love, truth and peace. The pain dissipates and understands what love truly means, it doesn't hurt anymore, when there is no more pain, there is only love.

Life is like a mystery, when you discover the truth life becomes a lighter path to tread on. Your heart becomes light and it helps others to see their own brightness when you radiate this bright light that comes from the Divine's heart of wisdom. The secret is love beyond form, dramas and suffering. We are here to experience love and happiness with all that is. Let us begin this path by unveiling what lies beyond our pain, let go of this suffering and surrender to your magnificent self.

The soul magnifies everything and allows this expansion to what is. Our hearts are like these vessels of love that longs to pour into our humanity to create the oneness of God's love and wisdom for us. There is no more pain but peace that is beyond the level of understanding that our mind can hold.

This inner peace is the foundation for letting go of our attachment to pain and suffering. When we connect to our stillness, we create a different pattern of life that holds a higher vibration of love and light. Thus, life becomes a reflection of God's love for us. We are the bearer of light and love. Unleash yourself from this pain that our humanity had gone through the ages.

The enlightenment is here and now.

Your heart and mind are aligned to what is and all is well. Forgive others and yourself to pave the way to healing. This lightens the load that you carry consciously or unconsciously in your essence. The path of the heart is through this doorway that opens once true forgiveness is attained. Love is rediscovering the full and highest potential of our existence, giving inspiration and enthusiasm to all sentient beings.

The shadows become light. There is understanding of the heart and mind and how they both align and become congruent to each other. This connection is needed to be in full alignment with the soul's purpose. The pain body is gone and just lives on love. It now attracts love and not fear because there is no more space for pain. The heart lives its desires and highest potential is clear and determine to be the force of life.

Love is power. It is the highest vibration of God's love for us. Let us connect to this power and our lives will be in a happy and peaceful state of condition. Letting go of illusions and fear is part of the process. Surrendering to the flow of life where it leads us. Most of the time we get used to the comfort zone and we find it hard to let go because of our attachments to things, places and people that we surround ourselves with. These attachments keep us inside the box and withhold our expansion. Our freedom lies in discovering our truth, which is our spirit.

The pain body that attracts another sentient being carrying the same energetic codes will give you the lessons in life that you seek. Once attained, your level of understanding will expand and now shift into a higher level of consciousness which is about love and light. The light quotient that you carry will increase and will see clearly why things have to happen that way. What is clearing will hold a vibration that is higher in frequency and that helps you elevate your consciousness. Allowing the flow of grace and ease to your energetic imprints will transform your inner being to its highest potential.

The heart has doorways to your expansive self that see no boundaries to what you want to experience. This doorway has the key to your soul. You hold the key to your happiness and inner peace. The pain is the key in disguise. Take the pain and see beyond it, transform yourself by understanding the underlying cause of this pain. Usually when you ask yourself, the answers will be revealed to you.

> *Face fear and heal with unconditional love for yourself.*

Ask yourself, "If I truly love myself, would I allow things that causes me harm? Would you be in the pattern of pain and suffering if you love yourself? What do you do, to let go of this pattern? Are you ready to clear this in your life? Did you learn the lesson? What is the lesson that life is revealing to you?" These are some questions that can help you clear what is not clear for you.

Tapping into your Akashic Records helps you clear your blockages and make you able to clear your energetic fields. This is working to empower you, and to attain your highest potential. When you unveil the pain in your heart, you receive the codes for healing and empowering your life. You tap into the Source and become at peace with yourself and others. The clearing is the removal of the thin veil that hinders your perception to what is. Once this is lifted, you now see the beauty that is within and to all sentient beings.

There is no separation but Oneness, feeling that you are at one in nature and all that is. Our pain is our compass towards total freedom of the spirit. Let us see this pain with a different outlook and use this as our tool to discover our true purpose and our heart's desires will show us our way.

Letting Go

Letting go of things that don't work like relationships that are toxic, work that you are not happy doing, friends that put you down, addictions, pain and suffering and many other things that you tend to cling to can be difficult, if we don't understand the level of our consciousness and how we got there in the first place. If everything, all matter, including yourself is energy and created in the nothingness, then all these entanglements are created in this non-local space. The question is how we can transform ourselves into new selves? Then we have to change from this field of consciousness because that is where we create our manifestations.

Clearing our energetic fields takes a lot of subtle queues to know if we are in alignment with our Higher

Self. It is meant to be simple because we are engineered to be intuitive and know what is good for us but because of all our human conditioning we are blinded by many hindrances. The map of our Consciousness guides us when we feel certain emotions that will tell us if we are creating things for our highest good. When we are in the downside of the scale, like experiencing fear, anxiety, negative emotions, then these feelings tell us that we are not in our best self.

Our natural Self is love and light because we are created in this vibration of fields. The shadows that we are experiencing are here to help us get the lessons in this lifetime. Be able to embrace the lessons and move forward. If we didn't learn the lesson then similar situations will come in different forms because we have not transformed our Consciousness. So changes can only occur when there is transformation in the Akashic fields. Our book of life will then record this and find a new pattern of your Akashic Records.

The pain and suffering of our existence is part of being a human. We live in a paradoxical world, but when are enlightened, we become One with everything and nothing. The attachments that we have to things, even people, will start to dissipate and we will find ourselves in a happy and peaceful state. The uncertainty of lives and what we can do now is what truly what matters.

There is no past. The present moment will be your blueprint in the future events that will take place in your chosen experiences. Miraculously and unexpectedly the Universe collaborates with your new choices and perceptions on how you view the world. Like living outside the box, you become One with the space. Be the observant of what you choose to see in your life experiences.

> To learn new experiences, we have to acknowledge
> them and see beyond the drama that we attract.

Remind yourself that everything is a reflection of yourself; the entanglement that is created is because something inside of you is a part of this manifestation. The shadows that you see are actually a part of you, with that, you can embrace this and see that everything is a lesson in the bigger picture. As long as you still blame, or see that the other people are separate from your Consciousness, you would not be able to let go. Letting go is actually essential in creating a new pattern of your new Self.

The expansion of your new self will manifest in many different ways. There will be joy within your heart, and people will be attracted to your presence. There is love that you emanate, and the loving kindness that you share for others will radiate the essence of your soul. Letting go of your old self and be the new Self that creates more love and light to our vast Universe. You are here to live beyond our old patterns of thinking, creating infinite possibilities and your highest potential.

Your soul is the creator of these physical experiences when your heart and mind are open to what is available. Aligning your mind into your heart that there is no limit to what you can experience. Start creating from this field of mind and heart Consciousness to bring into your realities things that support your Higher Self.

Letting go is creating space for infinite possibilities that you can experience as an awake and aware Conscious being. We become the observant of our realities and our life is the tapestry of our own creation and perception. This space that we attune to is the nothingness or the flow of the universal energy that creates accordingly to the frequency of our vibrations.

We are free-spirited beings that are here to experience life in multidimensional fields.

We are not constricted physical forms that experiences death and simply gone into ashes. We are more than this physical change, we are eternal like the Universe, and we are omnipresent in the cellular memories of others and ourselves. These memories are like collections of experiences, of which we are a part. The dance of these waves of energy, give us these continuing vibrations of life and death. Death is not permanent. It is a transition to another dimension of many other realms that we traverse.

Fear is the root of all attachment. When we let go of fear, we become free and truthful to our own existence. This fear only holds you into the depth of darkness and when someone stays there, freedom is lost. The fear of letting go is not going to bring you in any new door that will help you in your transition. Listen to your inner guidance, intuition and Higher Self. They are here to support and guide you in anything that is not in alignment with your soul. Experience love, peace and joy in your life even though it doesn't feel like that at the given moment. Once you transcend your Consciousness and see that everything is a reflection of what you needed to learn, then you can let go. Bring peace into your every breath and moments.

True Freedom

People are stuck in many ways when it comes to relationships. Relationships are mirrors of our self. The shadows that we have to face in others are actually our own shadows reflected back to us. It comes out when one has to face what the other person gives to us.

We are blinded by our expectations and illusions that when the truth is revealed, we blame the other person for the downfall of the relationship. We excuse our own selves from owning that we are actually a participant in this drama that we created. The only way to transcend this problem is to shift our Consciousness in becoming an observant of the drama. Accepting yourself where you are and start to see it in a different perspective.

There is a lot of stuck energy that is in the entanglement of toxic relationships, one is fear of being alone. Usually someone stays even though knowing that this bonding has no growth because of this comfort zone and fear of change. It is a co dependency to stay, not living your true self and freedom. When one has abandonment issue from childhood, it becomes the seed and pattern of broken relationships.

Rejection is an emotional trigger that creates pain and suffering, when one is abandoned, the walls around the heart create more separation. The continuing cycle of blame, guilt and anger persist in this bonding as there is no truth about owning once participation and responsibility for healing to take place. The strength and courage to move forward is not that easy to attain, because we all have excuses that we hold onto.

We don't see the light when we are in this deeply embedded darkness. All we see is the other person's fault and blame everything to the other person. Healing cannot take place where there is no forgiveness and knowing that what we see from the other person is what we need to heal within us. Our reflection is us and when we are in this field of consciousness and pure awareness we can see beyond the drama and suffering.

Awareness of consciousness is a step forward to true freedom from all toxic relationships.

When one becomes aware of the bigger picture, which is that everything that happens to you is deeply embedded within your Consciousness. Then we shift the energy to being empowered and not being the victim of circumstances. We self-realize when we have the power to create our realities based on shifting our consciousness. Being the observer of our own realities, we shift our experiences to being one with all that is. If we want to create true freedom, we have to be free from all separation and know that we are infinitely correlated and one in all. Anything we allow is created in our sub-conscious and thus manifest in our realities.

When you are in some situations that don't align within your mind and heart, ask the universe what is it that you need to know? Ask yourself this important self-reflective question, "If I love myself what would I be doing?" These questions will direct you in the path of true freedom of the spirit. Self-respect and self-love are the fruits of being an evolved sentient being.

You become one in every situation that arises in your fields of consciousness and energetically you align with the truth, love and light.

Chapter 3

ALIGNMENT OF OUR
EGO AND TRUE SELF

Merging our Ego and True Self

Our True Self is connected to the Source of all that is, when we are born, our consciousness creates our soul's desires and manifests our realities when we are aligned to our heart's intention. God is the universe, creation, universal energy and flow. You are a part of this creation, connected to the Source of life. Your soul is a breath of this life force that connects to all living beings and things. When you're aware of this universal self, you are one with the Source of creation. You become the creator and in Oneness with all the realities of your experiences in this multi-dimensional universal self that you are.

There are multi dimensions that we traverse and in this third dimension we are blinded by our attachments to the physical matter of things. We try to run away from our True Self to stay stuck in our worldly views and beliefs. When we are born, we tap into the collective consciousness of humanity. Our ego is born and creates our illusory self. This is our small self that holds our thought patterns and what we call voices in the head. We become alienated and separated from others believing that we are not like the rest of humanity. We build walls around our hearts therefore creating pain caused by our emotional traumas and mental tortures.

Embracing the shadows of humanity is part of being in Oneness.

When we learn to listen with our hearts open and become compassionate with what the other person is going through, we become a light in their path. The darkness of humanity is part of our duality. Transcending the aspect of this duality will bring light to our shadows and align us into our higher selves. The darkness is a void just like the worm holes in the Universe. The universe continually creates itself infinitely just like our True eternal self. We don't die but we continually recycle in our forms of light and consciousness. Our intentions create our realities here and now.

Our intention when align to our True Self, becomes an experience of joy and bliss. Awareness of ego and allowing ourselves to merge with all that is, holds the key to inner peace. Meditation plays an important role and practice in becoming aware of our thoughts. They release the attachments to our unconscious negative beliefs then, we become conscious of our thoughts and our emotions. They become the guide to our True self. When we hold the vibrations of love and light, we are in alignment with our higher selves.

Our heart is a true compass towards our ascension. Let it be our guide when in doubt of anything. The intuitive heart has the wisdom that holds your Truth. When you are true to yourself, you feel good, and it doesn't hold resistance in your emotional fields. The lower negative emotional state of our being is an indicator that we are not resonating with our higher self. Be aware of feelings and ask if this is for your highest good? The heart holds the wisdom of our soul and it is very simple to know, just ask and you shall receive it.

We stop reacting to others' negative energies. Know that these people need love and understanding. Instead of reacting, which indicates that you are still in the ego mode, you become centered and aware that you have a peaceful space you can occupy. This is the fruit of meditation and inner exploration of our soul journeys. We become one with all that is. Be a space of love and grace.

Going with the Flow

Going with the flow of life is the secret to happiness and simple joys of life. When you go with the flow, you are not resisting whatever is present in your realities. Whatever happens doesn't mean that you are going to sacrifice yourself and be in the cycle of victim consciousness, but be aware of where you are in your energetic fields. When you resist what is happening then the lesson is not yet learned, until we get the lesson, these situations are brought upon by the universe. This is the way how the universal laws work with us. We are in harmony with the movements of this universe, and what we resist persists.

> *Ask how you are going to release whatever is happening that is not for your highest good and potential.*

Things that happen are here to open your eyes to what is deeply embedded in your psyche and in the wounds of your soul. You will meet people that are completely different from your point of view and these are gifts to your awakening. When you truly listen and open your mind and heart to what they are talking about, you will find that you are all the same spirits experiencing how to be human with vulnerabilities and soft spots. We are here to learn not to judge anyone for their understanding. We can only love and see beyond the dramas that our humanity had created for eons of time. We are here to remember that we are bigger than this stuff. We are souls that can be what we want to be because we are powerful, limitless sentient beings.

When you're with someone, ask your Higher Self, what is the mirror of this situation in my life and what is the role that I'm partaking in this relationship? By asking you will find clarity of what is happening within and what the other person represents to you. Then, the "gift" is what you're supposed to learn and evolve in that pure loving essence that you are. If you find yourself stuck, ask if you can accept and allow this to be release in your Consciousness?

Opening ourselves can feel very vulnerable and difficult when you have created walls around your heart from being hurt again. Our ego thinks that this is good for us, denying us experiences that could have evolved into something beautiful. Get out of your head and go down to your heart and listen to what it is telling you. We are so busy with our thoughts that we rarely pay attention listening to our hearts. This is what is going on with our consciousness, we become our ego and we forget that our souls are far more important to be the source of everything that we want to manifest in our realities.

The freedom in learning your lesson is attuning yourself into your Higher Self. When you are in this space you become fearless, loving, happy and peaceful. Just like a rippling effect in the ocean, the people around you feel this and become unified with you. This is the unseparated consciousness of humanity that we are in right now. We live this in our daily lives and express this magnificent love and service to others. We are love and light.

Balancing your masculine and feminine energy, you will find clarity in your goals and dreams in life. The visions are more focus and your creations are manifesting in expansive ways. Allowing the flow of events in your life with awareness and tapping into your highest potential will give you the blissful space in your existence. Be what you want to be by allowing and surrendering to the flow of the divine energy that is within you and create a magnificent adventure of your soul's journey.

Allowing Unconditional Love to Grow

The space of unconditional love is where we want to be but it takes a lot of understanding, wisdom and growth to be in this lovely space. When we are growing as children, most of us have experiences that are abusive and detrimental to our emotional, mental and spiritual aspects of our being. We then carry these wounds of our souls into our cellular memories and consciousness. These are not easy to let go and heal without a spiritual guide and a healer because we are dealing with the soul level of our core being. We are not only physical bodies experiencing these painful traumas but we are souls that are wounded because of our pain. When we heal beyond the trauma, we reconnect to our soul and the heart of our Akashic Records. We rewrite our Soul Records and become evolve and enlighten to what our lessons are in this lifetime.

Things that matter in the healing process of wounded souls:

1. Sense of belonging is important to recognize when someone is in pain. The awareness that you are longing to have someone is a soft spot that will take deeper reflections on your healing and becoming more vulnerable to what is needed to be released. Going deeper to the pain of not belonging to someone and realizing this empty spot will help break open your heart to others for comfort and belonging. No one is an island, and truly we are never alone in the spiritual world but in this physical dimension we all want to be loved, touched and belong to someone with whom we can share our intimacy.

2. Fear of intimacy is the common factor in people who have problems with relationships due to painful events in their lifetime. Not being able to feel love unconditionally by their parents and others creates a wall that can surround their hearts to protect them from hurting. However, these walls also barricade them from experiencing unconditional love. It is a paradox of life, what you think will help you will also be the source of pain in the end. Fear is ego and when we let go of this fear and become open to what is happening, to trust the divine flow of our life, we will find that doors are actually opening to us to find this space of love. Awareness of this fear of intimacy will bring light and understanding why things didn't work for you. When you become aware of this issue, you have the power to turn it around and allow love to heal your broken heart and wounded soul.

3. Trust is surrendering to the unknown, which is allowing this loving energy to flow in your lifetime. When you trust with all your heart and soul, you become aware of the universal energy that all is taken care of and everything is well. Everything happens for a reason and the bigger picture will be revealed to you when you see beyond the pain, drama and chaos. You can only find this peaceful space when you surrender to God, whoever God is for you. This peace is beyond your understanding and only

the grace of the divine energy can heal your soul. Your mind can't heal with the same mind that created the problem as Einstein said. We need to transform the way we think, shifting our mind consciousness with love and trust.

4. Knowing that we are all One and that we have agreements with these people that hurt us in our soul's paths will help us see the bigger picture why things had to happen the painful way. When we have agreements in the spiritual realm just like an architect would have blueprints before building a project. It is like us in the spiritual realm, before we manifest here we have the blueprints of our souls. The biggest lesson in life is to learn forgiveness and unconditional love. Our family members and people that touched our lives or crossed our paths are our Sacred Contracts that help us in learning these lessons. Without them we would never be in this space of forgiveness and unconditional love. They have to show up in our dramas for us to learn and become a better person. When we see them like this, we become more compassionate and have the awareness that this is a part of our Sacred Contract. This is the only way a person can heal and see others as souls that are also healing. We are all one in spirit and body, when we hurt others we feel hurt. This oneness can be achieved when one is ready to let go and allow love to flourish and grow in their lifetime.

5. Compassion and kindness towards us is important in healing. People tend to be hard on them and they are unaware or unconscious about this because of our pain bodies. We carry these painful memories and suppress our emotions and feelings within our emotional bodies which then become toxic to our core being. Loving ourselves first is the secret to giving love to others. When we truly love ourselves, we don't allow harmful thoughts that will not be beneficial to us. We only allow good thoughts that will create good feelings and actions. We become connected to the Universal energy and flow of life with abundance, love and peace. This is our natural state which is unconditional love, we can be in this space when we flow with our truth, trust and surrender to the spirit of Oneness with forgiveness in our hearts and souls.

Doors Opening For Your Beautiful Self

Never in my wildest dreams that I will be in this peaceful place of my beautiful self where there is unconditional love for my true essence and core being of whom I am and what I am supposed to be. There is this awesomeness that I feel within my cellular existence that I am here to experience life and love with all that is. This lovely feeling stems from the Oneness that is here in our realities and multi-dimensional beings that we are. When we become conscious that we are one and that what we see is actually what we are inside, then we realize that this is the key that holds to true happiness.

If we are feeling separation from others, then this means we are still feeling some fragmentation in our consciousness.

If we take a look at this within and feel that separation where it resides in our consciousness, we will find the answers to our questions why we feel separated from others. We have to pay attention to our feelings and how we see others to guide us in how we can be in a space of oneness. Truly there is no separation, and we are all here to experience life in its fullest. Our troublemakers are our teachers so to speak, let's welcome these enemies with wide eyes wide open and see them as our keys to see within ourselves.

What are the ways to know you are feeling separation from others? The simplest way is to look at your relationships to see if there is any conflict and drama. This will tell you for sure that there are some deep introspective issues that you need to look within yourself. Others are just mirrors of what you need to work on obviously if we are One, then what we see that others are doing wrong is exactly what we have inside ourselves that needs healing and integration. When we acknowledge this aspect in us then this awareness will create an alignment within our energy centers that will open doors for our consciousness to expand and open doors for our beautiful selves to radiate and shine.

Life is a creation and we are co-creators with the universal energy. We have the power to create anything we want when we align ourselves with this knowing. Allowing only what makes us feel good and not reacting to things that harm us is wisdom. Releasing the past and letting go of thoughts that do not resonate with love will take you to a peaceful state of mind. Meditation is an important practice in self-awareness. It gives you awareness that the thoughts in your head are just thoughts that pass by and that you don't need to identify with them. These thoughts when they vibrate in negative frequency, will give you situations that are disempowering, therefore being aware of your negative thoughts is a step in empowerment.

The mind and heart needs to be aligned to create wholesomeness. The doors of your heart are the keys to the treasures in this lifetime. When you open the door to positive thoughts in life, it will create miracles along the way. Imagine there are two doors in the gate of your heart; one door stays closed for things that are harmful and the other door remains open for good things. These doors are the gatekeepers of your creation. As long as you envision these doors, you will be wise to know that there is a gatekeeper for your heart and your life will manifest your beautiful self.

Allowing, and going with the flow of life, creating miracles along the way, you will find bliss in your lifetime. Opening your mind and heart to allow this space will manifest your paradise here on Earth. It will take you to experiences beyond your imagination. Your dreams will come true and your life will be filled with people that love and support you just like the universe is saying you are loved. There are no limits to what you can create. The fire in your heart will continue to ignite the passion that you are here to create. Tap into your highest potential creating a life that is heaven here on Earth. Open the doors of your heart and live your life to the fullest by experiencing the beauty and love within.

Acceptance and Allowing the Flow of Life

There are blockages that hinder us from being happy, peaceful and content when we resist things that don't work. When things are given to us by the Universe in situations that don't make sense, we become defensive and go into our fearful mode. When we are so busy with the external drama, we are consumed with don't even exist in the present moment. We go into fear mode and create more anxieties for ourselves. Rather than stopping and creating solutions we become reactors to the chaos. Only when we stop analyzing why things happen, we become an observer of the situation and we connect to our heart space that lies within the wisdom of our souls.

If we are wise, we will not allow our mind to think of harmful thoughts, but what do we do? We become unconscious of our thoughts especially when we are facing some problems. The secret for us is to always go into our heart space where this wisdom seats. Thoughts can give us realizations where we need clarity and our heart can give us the answer to our questions. Deep within our energetic blueprints and our subconscious mind creates situations that are in our realities. Asking our Akashic Records where these are hidden from our consciousness can help us transcend anything that blocks us from our True Selves.

In our past, incarnated historic lives, and unconscious negative beliefs about ourselves and others, unhealed emotions and energetic cords of lower vibratory frequency can create cycles or patterns of relationships that we have. When we become aware of their roots, then we can heal them with new pathways of energetic patterns of our Consciousness. The Sacred form of Merkabah will help you in creating a safe and sacred space for your healing. Opening your Akashic Records and asking where you need some healing and guidance.

In healing, there are signs in recognizing when healing itself becomes an attachment or addiction. When someone doesn't stop seeking, it is a sign that the individual is stuck in the pain body. Because truly there is nothing to heal, the healer is within you when you realized that God is within you. When one realizes this, then the seeking will dissipate. There is only love, peace, happiness and contentment. It is difficult to see one self when they are in the cycle of healing, because the healer needs to heal thyself. The roles that we do are not us, but our ways that we convey our service to humanity. When we can't see beyond our work, they become a false identification of our true selves. Our truth is just love. When we love ourselves, our love shines through others and they recognize their own love and light. We are here to experience love and give light. Our identification with our work and even service to humanity is just a fragment of our ego and archetypal energy.

Our truth is beyond the situations in which we are involved. Acceptance and allowing what is given to us in the flow of our lives will guide us to what we need to let go and love. We are more than our eyes can see and what we can feel. Our existence is beyond multi-dimensional fields of our energetic blueprints. When we know our truth, anything is in resonance to our highest selves. We vibrate in the frequency of love and light. We attract situations that are in these vibrations and create more loving, harmonious, peaceful and blissful relationships for us and others.

Allowing is releasing that is not good for us.

Our roles in our participation in the relationships will give us glimpses of where we need to let go or choose to love. Let go of fear, and allow love to be with you in your choices. Self love is the first in our list when we want to move forward in our lifetime. When we truly love ourselves, we only allow loving relationships. We become sensitive to how we feel and what others bring into our relationships. Opening our hearts and trusting is allowing the universal energy to flow and bring to our lives abundance, peace and bliss. Let us connect and align to the beauty that lies within our hearts and know that our creations are co creations of our hearts and souls for our highest good and all sentient beings.

May the light of this beautiful heart bring pure love and shining light to help you see the love and light within yourself.

Chapter 4

ACTIVATION OF THE
UNIVERSAL SELF

The Power of Forgiveness

Forgiveness is the foundation of healing. When we forgive, we create a space of unconditional love and grace. The pathway to Oneness is connected through this force. Without this bridge, we will not achieve inner and global peace. As we forgive others for what they done to us, we literally transcend our vibrations. We start to attract more unconditional love and blessings into our lives. The power of this action is beyond measure. There is a rippling effect that happens when we choose to do this. We magnify our existence, and manifest lovely experiences in our lifetime.

> *We learn to let go of the past and pain, and heal*
> *our cellular memories and consciousness.*

The Universe will surely test us. It will trigger more unforgiveness until we truly get the lesson behind a situation, which is unconditional love. The hidden gem is all about our love for our self. If we truly love ourselves, we will not allow thoughts that will harm us in any way. When we withhold love, we create lower vibration emotions like guilt, anger, revenge, resentment, and anxiety within our consciousness.

Without self love, we create stress in our health and being. We become hard on ourselves and create armour around our hearts. Our hearts then become a perfect ground to breed unwanted feelings and negative emotions. These emotions rut in our hearts. Our souls become stuck in the darkness. We become victims of our own consciousness. When this happens we are separated from our Source, which is about love, unity and harmony.

We are not here to experience pain and suffering, but to be in the space of love and grace. We forget who we are. We are spiritual beings in our human suits. All of our dramas are our own creations, because we attract who we are inside our hearts. When we see beyond our pain, and see the bigger picture, we will know that we are all on the same boat. We experience these situations in different forms. The question is, "Do we ever get the lessons that we are trying to learn?" We all have conscious choices to make this lifetime. We can live a happy life or be stuck in negative situations within ourselves and others. Let us wake up and take responsibility for the state of our consciousness.

> *Blaming others for our state of mind is not going to help us in the present moment.*

Like the bite of a snake, the snake is long gone but we still suffer its venom. We are caught in the poison of the snake. This is the venom of the unforgiveness path. We create more pain by holding this crooked path in our existence. The garden of our hearts is like a landscape. We need to weed out bad weeds, like ill feelings and grudges in order to reap good fruits in our harvest. Forgiving the past is not easy.

But if we want to move forward, we must choose to forgive and let go of the past. Focus on your chosen path and follow your heart. This is the return home. Your heart is where your home is. This is our Sacred Contract. It allows us to be with certain people so we can experience pain and forgiveness. Looking at the bigger picture, without this situation we will not learn the lesson of forgiveness.

When we start to see things as they are and send blessings to the enemy, so to speak, inner peace will be found deep within our hearts. We feel light and in the space of grace and Divine's love. Only through the dark nights of our soul, can we achieve true forgiveness and learn the lesson. If we keep denying our own pain and blame others for how we feel, we will just go in a circle of drama. Then we keep attracting the same situation with different actors, so to speak.

> *We transcend our pain by forgiving and letting go*
> *of the negative karma.*

Allow the space and power to heal your heart. We become co-creators of our lovely and happy experiences. We choose to empower ourselves, and allow ourselves to expand into this beautiful creation of God, for whatever God means to us. We learn to trust the flow of love in our experiences. We become happier in our existence when we connect to our soul's Akashic Records.

This is the secret path to tap into the Akashic Records. We cannot touch this when we have no forgiveness in our existence. This is because the heart of our human collective consciousness is in the realm of our souls. We can only go through our soul's high vibration, if we connect to the Source of our existence.

Our souls vibrate in the frequency of love and light, so we have to be aligned and congruent with our souls to access the Akashic Records. People are mistaken if they think that they have to be smart in order to access their Akashic Records. It is actually the heart that needs to be pure, to access the high frequency of vibration of love and light. God sees us beyond our mind's perceptions. It is within our hearts which lays the wisdom of our Source. This is the path of our return to home, which is where love is.

There is no sense in holding pain, anger, and resentment in our existence, because we only give ourselves a more difficult path to tread. Let us forgive ourselves first to experience true forgiveness for others. We don't need to be with them, except to allow the space for love and grace within our being. This creates a new pattern of experiences. Then we become more aligned to manifest our dreams this lifetime. Let us live in the present moment, consciously choosing to forgive.

> *"I now declare to the Universe and Source that I'm forgiving others who consciously or unconsciously have hurt me in the past. I also ask others to forgive me for hurting them consciously*

or unconsciously through my thoughts, words and
actions. Let it be done. May the flow of grace and
love be with me in this lifetime. Amen."

The Fruits of Unconditional Love

Unconditional love is a fruit of purification. This happens within the soul's journey in being human. This means undergoing a process of purifying negative thoughts from your mental fields, toxic emotions, and emotions that calibrate low in the map of consciousness. Clearing your consciousness with the energy of love. So with this process, you clear your Consciousness to the present moment.

Remove blockages that stop you from being your highest potential. Release unforgiveness from the heart. Release unconscious negative beliefs in your cellular memory and cellular tissues. Release unresolved Karmic bonds from family, lineage, and DNA levels of cellular memory and consciousness. Heal the soul and access your Akashic Records, to create a space of grace and unconditional love.

The soul's evolution is transcending human consciousness into the Divine's heart of unconditional love and wisdom. There are stages of development that we go through as human beings before achieving a level of enlightenment and inner peace. We must undergo a lot of detachments from all things, relationships, and other worldly attachments. This is called detoxification.

The space that we clear becomes empty. It is now ready to be the vehicle of light. From this, the Merkabah can now travel freely and connect to your being. Our physical existence protects and holds our light body. When we are in pain, our body is telling us energetically that we are carrying toxins. This is where every body part can manifest illness.

This is how we use the Chakra Energy centers to detect which issues we are going through. It detects which dynamics of energy we need to heal and release blockages. We are made of vibration waves of light particles. Love is the magnifying life force that holds us here in our existence. It is the Source of our creation that holds our blueprint. When we were created in our mother's womb, we hold our soul's blueprints. It is given to us, manifesting the grand creations of God.

> *We are being energetically linked to the Divine's*
> *Soul of love and wisdom.*

We have to fill the void with unconditional love, from the Divine. Then we can see and feel love for ourselves and others. Our human conditioning prevents us from fully accessing our Divine self. We are not alone in our soul's journey. So ask and you shall receive.

When asking for healing and guidance, we are spiritually guided in our higher dimension. Our Akashic Records evolve as we transform into more loving and enlightened beings. When aligning your physical, mental, emotional, spiritual and soul bodies of your existence, you expand and magnify in a blissful state of co-creation with the Divine's love and wisdom.

The Stages or process of clearing for unconditional love:

1. Awaken from painful situations that you may have. In drama or suffering, become aware that everything is energy and that relationships are your mirrors. This is the victim consciousness, the Archetypes of: Saboteur, Victim, Prostitute and Child. These serve as catalysts for your transformation and shift. See the signs. Listen to your dreams and guides for deeper reflection on what's happening.

   Take full responsibility for attracting these situations. You also need to clear more subtle bodies that are not in alignment with your bright soul. Just like a diamond in a rough, you need this perfect brilliance to become a vehicle of light to others and the Universe. Have clarity, inner strength, and courage to move on by forgiving yourself and others.

2. Be aware of your soul's purpose. This is a fire that continually ignites your being. At this stage, you become an observer of your situations. Start practicing meditation and healing. Pay attention and listen to your body, mind, and emotions. Ground your soul's purpose. You realize that

you are not about work, and become less attached to what the world's affairs are going through.

Open your Third Eye Chakra to see beyond the veil. The truth sets you free, so let go of attachments. You become aware of your bigger purpose and service to humanity. This can be anything from your creative nature, healing others, helping children, being a writer, being a mentor to others, advocating for victims, or anything that makes you happy and brings out your passion. See your Archetypal energy patterns. These are your guides that can compass you to your destination.

3. Align to your soul's purpose through a process of connecting to your spiritual guides, balancing and clearing your Chakra Energy Centers. Align your physical, mental, emotional, spiritual and soul levels of your body into your present moment. All energy fields will be cleared at this stage. Challenges will come as grounds for empowerment. Bring the transmission of Divine's unconditional love and light into your blueprint. This is your Akashic Records, linking to all that is and the collective consciousness of humanity. Let us shift to a new paradigm from victimhood into empowerment.

4. Ascend and activate your DNA, cellular tissues, fibres, memories, and consciousness into Divine's love and wisdom. Remember, your home is where your heart is. Let us shift from "me" to "we." Energetically link to the Ascended Masters, Archangels and angels, Saints and spiritual guides for protection, healing, support, direction, clarity and guidance.

Return to home. This is your soul's access to your Akashic Records and others. Be a vehicle of unconditional love and light. Manifest and co-create Paradise in your fields. Experience Heaven on Earth. Transcend lower vibrations of emotions into love and peace. Then your presence will dissipate darkness and negative energy, becoming one with the Source and all sentient beings.

Inner Peace

Inner peace is attained when one has Stillness in the mind and happiness in the heart. It is the space that permeates all individual cells of existence, and feels that they are one in the collective consciousness of humanity. There is only space of love instead of fear or separation with others or other species. This is the essence of all that is. One can only attain inner peace when the individual recognizes the insanity or madness of the mind and becomes an observer of these incessant thoughts of the ego. The person watches the drama that one projects, when attached to the little self in the head that continually speaks to make its existence known because of fear of annihilation. The recognition of this illusion is the awakening that happens within one's own psyche and self-realized that there is only this moment of now and aliveness within the body that is present right now. The thoughts that are in the past or future are not here and are part of the dysfunctions of the human conditioning and beliefs.

The searching or seeking of Enlightenment comes into stillness and one knows that there is nothing to search for anymore but to enjoy their lifetime and start being whoever and wherever they are. Life becomes more colourful and vibrant, alive in their relationships with others and one in nature. There is a field of unity or unified Consciousness within itself and others. It sees beyond drama and form, beyond what life presents, takes challenges with flow of ease and grace. The flow of life becomes more fluid and light. It is the peace beyond the level of understanding, surpasses words, thoughts, and become what is. The silence within and infinite immortality which is eternal presence of the spirit and soul. In attaining inner peace one creates a rippling effect in the collective consciousness of humanity towards Universal peace.

We are the fragmented part of the universal energetic hologram. Anything we put out in the universe is being received and echoed out to the Universe, this is the law of Karma. When one is aware of the causality of their behaviour one becomes responsible for everything and thus creates synchronized events that will lead them to their inner knowing and self-realization. Everything is a mirror of itself. It is a reflection of how we see ourselves and the inner landscapes of our life garden. Weeding out our garden helps in our growth as a conscious human being. When we treat others as ourselves, we become one with the creation.

The space that is still is the silence in our hearts and mind. It is when nothing is conveyed or nothing to search anymore. There is no seeking or searching but just is. The breath is the bridge to this space, when you put your attention to your breath you allow your essence to bloom like a flower in your heart. The being becomes you and the doing part becomes null. Suddenly there is an alignment between your mind and heart. They become one in love and light, connecting to the vastness of the universe and cosmic energy. You become connected to all that is; aligned, awake and aware to what is happening in the universal fields.

When you are at peace with yourself, others become
you and you see them with eyes of loving kindness.

There is no separation between you and the rest of humanity. We are all one living organism, creating our multi-dimensional selves tapping into the vast expansive limitless universe. When we see our existence as one unified field, we develop compassion and kindness in our hearts for others. This is the path of a true spiritual warrior. Where there is darkness, we bring light and it dissipates the darkness into the world. This helps others to transcend their soul's journey with truth and light.

Our true soul's purpose is to ascend in this lifetime, to be one with our Source or God whatever that is for you. This physical lifetime can shift when you choose to do so. It is a free will to choose love rather than fear. This love will evolve to unconditional love when we become detach to all illusions in life. The veil will be lifted and wake us up into our truth, which is our spirit. There is no easy path, but to go through the purging and weeding out of these blockages that are hindering us to shine brightly. There is always light and our choice is to choose this path and calling of our souls.

The Awakening that is happening with our collective consciousness is here to tell us what choices make sense and what will lead us to our happiness and inner peace. It is simple yet we complicate this when we live inside the box. Let us align our mind and hearts together to be in this space of inner peace and knowing. Let us come together as one conscious family, align, awake and aware of our intentions to bring peace into this word and be conscious of our responsibility to choose peace. This is the shift in our consciousness to be a conscious being bringing love and peace within and outside our energetic fields. This will create a rippling effect to the vast and expansive universal fields. The Enlightenment times are here let us celebrate this every moment of our lifetime and together we can join in this Universal Conscious intention to create a future of hope, love and light.

The Light Activation of God's Love

We are here to radiate and shine God's light and love for us, to help others see their own light. As mirrors of God's reflections we see others souls as essence of God's love for us. We are here to experience love in our core being, because of our physical density, DNA makeup from our past ancestors and lineage, cellular memories and consciousness, we forget our Divine light. When we were created, God wanted infinitesimal fragments of God's souls which are all of us. This light that holds the love vibrations of God in our core being and essence is the spirit of God's breath in our physical body. We are made of multidimensional layers of energy and light particles that contain the crystalline fields of our molecular anatomy. The microcosm and macrocosm of our existence in the universal mind of God is omniscient, omnipotent and omnipresent. We are Divine beings of light and love when we align and activate our consciousness with the Divine's blueprint for our existence. Activating this Divine energy in our core being, aligning our mind and hearts together, opening the Chakra energy centers, transcending our consciousness with forgiveness and unconditional love for all sentient beings, we become one with God's love for us. We will see beyond the veil and feel love, peace, joy and bliss in our existence. Our experiences are going to be of love not from fear. We are the observers of what is manifesting in our fields and know that we have the power to shift anything that needs light. Problems don't affect us anymore, they become windows of opportunities for us to explore. We are the masters of our experiences, choosing love rather than fear.

> *Forgive your enemies as they are shadows of your soul.*

When you are able to forgive, you are able to accept these shadows in your essence. You become fully in love with all aspects of yourself, just love no judgement, live fully as is, laugh with joy and dance your life away. Life is a creation with the Divine's Sacred dance and rhythm of God's love for us. We are One with our Sacred lives in everything that we think, say or do. Life is Sacred, precious gift and manifestation of God's love for us. This space is available for all of us when we attune to this Divine energy within us. We are able to dissipate darkness with our light and help others see their light.

Humanity is going through a major shift and transition into this light consciousness. We are shifting to our multidimensional state of our consciousness. Our energy and vibrational frequency is shifting with mother Earth's changes within the planetary, universal and cosmic alignments that is happening in our fields. We are nurtured by the sun and we grow within connecting our light into this nourishing glow of the magnificent sun. Our moon is our emotional body that connects us to the floodgates of our hearts. It reflects and affects us in our emotional and mental fields. The planetary movements affect our archetypal and astrological birth dates. When we are born, we receive these archetypal and planetary blueprints of our souls. As everything is connected in space and energy so is our existence in the universal fields. There is no time and space in this soul continuum, when you live in your multidimensional state of being. You become the anchor of this light for others. You magnetize beautiful experiences when you are grounded and shine your light to others.

Creation is an important part of your existence. To create with your heart's desires with passion is your gift to humanity. Everyone is designed to create their soul's blueprint. The question is, "Are you ready to create your highest potential?" When you create, it is the heart that magnifies this manifestation. Your passion and attention will determine the result but without action, the universe will remain in suspension. Intention will collapse this suspension and create action. The activation of your light consciousness will connect you into the full embodiment of your soul's purpose. What are you waiting for? This life is yours, create, expand, and shine your bright light in the universal fields of God's love for you and others.

Universal Conscious Self

We are multidimensional light beings living in many parallel lifetimes. It takes awakening, awareness, alignment and activation of these energetic fields for expansion of one's conscious self to connect to the universe to be attune into this magnitude of vibratory frequency. When we are asleep to our existence, we become blind to our belief systems, unconscious negative beliefs, cellular memories and Consciousness of our past traumatic events in our lifetimes. Our veil is not lifted and the physical reality is the only dimension that makes sense. We are beyond this physical reality; we are expansive, multi-dimensional, energetically link to all sentient beings and mother Earth and multi universes.

Our earth has a protection around its ionosphere and earth's surface called the Schumann Resonance which has the frequency of approximately 7.83 Hz. Our brain also has the same wave frequency in Alpha meditative state which is interesting to know. Like our planet Earth, our human body has energy fields and we can ask for protection around us with thoughts and invocation of our Ascended Masters and light beings. When we are awake, we can envision or call this light around us for protection and clearing shadows, negative thoughts and energy.

Everything is energy. Thoughts become energy, and energy into action. When we open our crown chakra energy center, which sits on top of our head, we receive the universal and cosmic light that activates the Kundalini to rise. This energy can be awakened and it sits in front of the spine right to the perineum or root chakra energy center, it is very important to ground this energy to Earth. Our neuropath ways become activated, and that is why we need to be grounded, so we don't fry our brain cells. The correlation between the Schumann Resonance and our brain Alpha state indicates that when we stand on earth, the frequency is transmitted to our body system and our brain receives the same electromagnetic fields like the earth. We align to the Kundalini energy which is conducted when we open our crown chakra and receive the Universal and cosmic light. We have to anchor this energy into Mother Earth Gaia to manifest our soul's purpose and heart's desires.

This is the pathway of energy healers, they are Awakened to this energy and become conduits for others to receive this light and energy in their energy fields. Once Awakened and veil is lifted, the Awareness will bring manifestations of your intentions. Everything is connected to the source of love and light. You will be showing the effortless ways to be in the space of unconditional love and peace. The seeking for Enlightenment dissipates and you are aligned to everything in forms, sound, light and energy. You will develop heightened awareness of your intuition and psychic abilities. There is no fear, shadow or darkness only love and light. Everyone is a soul that is a gift from the Universe for you to know or explore. Every soul becomes an essence of unconditional love. You become an instrument for peace and calmness in the space where you are.

The shift that we are in, is about our Consciousness and our Universal Conscious self. When we awaken to our connection to the source of everything, we become empowered and we help others transcend their sufferings in this physical lower vibration of our dense third dimensional bodies. We become the instruments for their remembrance of where they came from. We are from the Universe and we are the Universe. Every molecular structure and cellular tissues of our physical bodies have the same sub-atomical particles of the Universe.

Our Archetypal energies that we carry in this lifetime direct us toward our passion and creations. When we open our Akashic Records, we have the access to these blueprints. We realize our mission here, opening our gates to heaven. Paradise is here, we create it in every conscious thoughts and vibratory frequency that we carry in our energetic fields. Be aware of what vibrations you are bringing into your space. Check in and ask yourself, Am I vibrating in love and light? Or am I in shadow or darkness. Shadows are just space that lacks light or love. When we are aware of what Consciousness we have, we can clear this with the energy of love and light. We have the power to shift anything, circumstances and situations. We are the alchemist in our laboratory of our thoughts, emotions and actions.

> *As we evolve, expand and enlighten our mind, body, heart, spirit and soul we align to the universal mind of God.*

The universal energy that we connect will give us wisdom and the love for our planet Earth will give us compassion toward all sentient beings. This will give us Oneness in all that is. There will be no separation or war. For us to reach this level of Enlightenment, we have to awaken ourselves first then we can help others. When we take away the judgment that we put on ourselves, we can be non judgmental about others. We need to be compassionate about ourselves because without this we can not love others unconditionally. We will become Universal Conscious Selves when Oneness in the unified consciousness becomes our intention for healing of humanity and our Mother Earth.

Contact Information

For more information, please contact Teza at:

Website: www.thepurpleoasis.com

YouTube: tezamysticangel

Facebook: Teza Zialcita

Twitter: tezamysticangel

Blog: www.hummingbird-isanybodythere.blogspot.com

Meetup.com: (search for) Star Lotus, Ascension

Email Address: thepurpleoasis@gmail.com

About the Author

Teza Zialcita is a certified Akashic Records Healer, Spiritual Writer and Teacher who is here to help others transcend their lives into oneness and create a sacred space that will connect them to the Source. She is a wounded healer in this lifetime and as a victim of sexual abuse she was able to transcend this experience to help others in their healing.

She believes every one of us have an innate ability to heal and she serves as a conduit for healing to manifest. Everything is energy and when we radiate a high frequency of love and light we connect to our highest potential and our Source.

Zialcita says our deepest healing is through our Akashic Records as we tap into our Book of Life, it will reveal to us our true soul's purpose and heart's desires. Without this knowledge and wisdom it will be difficult to remember our home. That's why she heard the words "You are returning to home," before she entered the studies of the Akashic Records and truly, this is the home where our soul resides. All of our DNA memories and consciousness are stored and kept in our Records.

Her intention is to reach the mass unconscious state of humanity for healing and to bring them into alignment to truth and Source. She intends to touch souls who are in the dark and bring light in their path. To serve, share, and be conscious enlightened beings in our thoughts, words and deeds in the present moment is her aim.